Cambridge Young Learners English Tests

Cambridge Flyers 4

Answer Booklet

Examination papers from

University of Cambridge

ESOL Examinations:

English for Speakers of Other Languages

CAMBRIDGE
UNIVERSITY PRESS

CAMBRIDGE UNIVERSITY PRESS
Cambridge, New York, Melbourne, Madrid, Cape Town, Singapore, São Paulo

Cambridge University Press
The Edinburgh Building, Cambridge CB2 2RU, UK

www.cambridge.org
Information on this title: www.cambridge.org/9780521611381

First published 2005
Reprinted 2005

Printed in Italy by Legoprint S.p.A.

A catalogue record for this publication is available from the British Library

ISBN-13 978-0-521-61138-1 Answer Booklet
ISBN-10 0-521-61138-5 Answer Booklet

ISBN-13 978-0-521-61137-4 Student's Book
ISBN-10 0-521-61137-7 Student's Book

ISBN-13 978-0-521-61139-8 Cassette
ISBN-10 0-521-61139-3 Cassette

ISBN-13 978-0-521-61140-4 Audio CD
ISBN-10 0-521-61140-7 Audio CD

Contents

Introduction

The *Cambridge Young Learners English Tests* offer an elementary-level testing system for learners of English between the ages of 7 and 12. The tests include 3 key levels of assessment: *Starters*, *Movers* and *Flyers*.

Flyers is the third level in the system. Test instructions are very simple and consist only of words and structures specified in the syllabus.

The complete test lasts about one hour and a quarter and has the following components: Listening, Reading and Writing, and Speaking.

	length	number of parts	number of items
Listening	approx. 25 minutes	5	25
Reading and Writing	40 minutes	7	50
Speaking	approx. 7 – 9 minutes	4	–

Candidates need a pen or pencil for the Reading and Writing paper, and coloured pens or pencils for the Listening paper. All answers are written on the question papers.

Listening

In general, the aim is to focus on the 'here and now' and to use language in meaningful contexts. In addition to multiple choice and short answer questions, candidates are asked to use coloured pencils to mark their responses in one task. There are 5 parts. Each part begins with a clear example.

Part	skill focus	input	expected response	number of items
1	listening for lexical items and verb phrases	picture and dialogue	matching names to figures in a picture by drawing lines	5
2	listening for specified information	gapped text (form to complete) and dialogue	recording words or numbers	5
3	listening for information	pictures and short monologues	matching pictures by writing a letter in a box	5
4	listening for information which identifies the correct picture	picture sets and dialogues	3-option multiple choice (pictures; tick the box for the correct picture)	5
5	listening for lexis and position	picture and dialogue	carrying out instructions; locating, colouring, drawing and writing correctly	5

Reading and Writing

Again, the focus is on the 'here and now' and the use of language in meaningful contexts where possible. To complete the test, candidates need a single pen or pencil of any colour. There are 7 parts, each starting with a clear example.

Part	skill focus	input	expected response	number of items
1	understanding definitions	word set and set of definitions	matching definitions to a picture	10
2	understanding short texts	1 picture 7 sentences	writing 'yes' or 'no' next to the sentences	7
3	identifying appropriate utterances	short dialogues with multiple responses	selecting best response by circling a letter	5
4	reading writing	story-cloze with picture prompts	gap-filling (prompted); one-word answers; choose the best title (Tick a box)	6
5	reading writing	story presented through 3 texts with 7 questions	writing 1–4-word answers to questions	7
6	understanding use of grammar and lexis	gapped text and word sets	completing text by selecting the best word and copying	10
7	understanding use of grammar and lexis	gapped text	writing words in gaps	5

Speaking

In the Speaking Test, the candidate speaks with 1 examiner for about 8 minutes. The format of the test is explained in advance to the child in their native language, by a teacher or person familiar to them. This person then takes the child into the exam room and introduces them to the examiner.

Speaking ability is assessed according to various criteria, including comprehension, the ability to produce a prompt, appropriate and accurate response, and pronunciation.

Part	input	expected response
1	greeting and name check (unassessed); 2 similar pictures (1 unseen) and oral statements about the unseen picture	identifying 6 differences between pictures
2	1 set of facts and 1 set of question cues	answering and asking questions about 2 people, objects or situations
3	picture sequence which outlines a story	relating a story
4	open-ended questions about the candidate	answering questions

Further information

The topics, structures, words and tasks upon which the *Cambridge Young Learners English Tests* are based are comprehensively described in the Handbook, so teachers or parents can know exactly what to expect.

Further information about the *Cambridge Young Learners English Tests* can be obtained from the Local Secretary for Cambridge ESOL examinations in your area, or from:

Cambridge ESOL
1 Hills Road
Cambridge
CB1 2EU
United Kingdom

Telephone: +44 1223 553997
Fax: +44 1223 460278
e-mail: ESOLHelpdesk@ucles.org.uk
www.CambridgeESOL.org

Test 1 Answers

William Sarah Harry Micheal Fred Helen Emma

purple

The Lake

green

yellow

blue

Listening

Part 1 (5 marks)

Lines should be drawn between:

1 Emma and the girl with the dinosaur on her T-shirt
2 Harry and the boy sitting inside the cave
3 Michael and the boy winning the race, in striped shorts
4 William and the boy painting a picture of an octopus
5 Helen and the girl on the blanket writing a letter

Part 2 (5 marks)

1 November 2 May 3 February 4 Autumn 5 Cumbline (correct spelling)

Part 3 (5 marks)

1 Tennis player – E 2 Mechanic – C 3 Policewoman – F 4 Doctor – H 5 Businessman – D

Part 4 (5 marks)

1 B 2 A 3 C 4 B 5 B

Part 5 (5 marks)

1 Colour the girl's plate – blue
2 Colour the smallest hill – purple
3 Draw a flower in the bottle on the table and colour it yellow
4 Write the word 'Lake' on the swan picture
5 Colour the telephone on the shelf – green

TRANSCRIPT *Hello. This is the Cambridge Flyers Practice Listening Test, Test 1.*

Part 1 *Listen and look. There is one example.*

[pause]

GIRL: Look at this photograph. I took it yesterday. It's good, isn't it?
MAN: It is, yes. It's excellent, but I don't know all the people in it.
GIRL: Oh, don't you? Well, you know Sarah. Look, there she is on the beach – she's making a castle.
MAN: Is she the girl who's putting the green flag on the top?
GIRL: Yes, that's right.

[pause]

Can you see the line? This is an example. Now you listen and draw lines.

[pause]

1

MAN: So who's the other girl with her?
GIRL: The one who's helping her to make the castle?
MAN: Yes, that one.
GIRL: It's my best friend, Emma. And look, she's wearing her favourite dinosaur T-shirt. She always wears it on the beach.

[pause]

2

MAN: The weather was nice, wasn't it?
GIRL: Yes it was. It was lovely. But my friend Harry doesn't like the sun very much, so he went into that cave.
MAN: Is that him, there – near the cave – the boy in the orange shorts?
GIRL: That's right. No, no sorry, I'm wrong. He's the boy who's *inside* the cave. It wasn't so hot in there.

[pause]

3

MAN: Those two boys had a good time that day, didn't they?

GIRL: Oh, those two, yes. They had a kind of competition, a race on the beach.
MAN: So who won the race?
GIRL: Michael did – the boy in the striped shorts. He's good at all kinds of sports.

[pause]

4

MAN: Do you like the two paintings?
GIRL: Well, the picture of the sky is lovely. But the other one – the one of the octopus – is horrible!
MAN: Oh, I like it. It's interesting. Who's the person painting it?
GIRL: I'm not sure. Is his name Fred? No, I'm sorry – it's his brother, William. They've both got the same curly hair.

[pause]

5

GIRL: Helen's brother has just gone to college. Look, she's writing a letter to him.
MAN: Are you sure? I can't see her.
GIRL: There, look. She's sitting on the blanket with her friend.
MAN: Oh, I see. She's the girl in the yellow T-shirt with the black spots.

[pause]

Now listen to Part 1 again.

[The recording is repeated.]

[pause]

That is the end of Part 1.

[pause]

Part 2 *Listen and look. There is one example.*

[pause]

WOMAN: Oh hello. I work for a children's magazine and I'm writing something about children and the different times of the year. Would you like to answer some questions for me?
BOY: Well, yes, if I can.
WOMAN: Thank you. OK, first, can you give me your name, please?
BOY: Yes, of course. It's Ben – Ben Perry. And that's P-E double-R-Y.

[pause]

Can you see the answer? Now you listen and write.

[pause]

WOMAN: Right. Thank you, Ben. Now, when's your birthday? I mean, which month?
BOY: My birthday? Why?
WOMAN: It's interesting. People usually like their birthday month.
BOY: Do they? Well I don't like mine very much. It's November.
WOMAN: Oh right. Let me write that here. Now perhaps you can tell me the month you like best. Which is your favourite month?
BOY: Mmm… I prefer May, I think. Yes, it's

lovely then. It's warm and sunny and we often go swimming.
WOMAN: OK, fine. Now, which month is the worst? What about January?
BOY: Well, I don't like it very much – but the month I *hate* is February. It's always cold and it rains a lot so we can't play outside very often.
WOMAN: But in some countries it's warm and sunny then, you know.
BOY: Yes, I know! But not here!
WOMAN: Now, do you usually have a holiday in the summer, Ben?
BOY: No. All my friends do, but my dad has to work then. So we have our holiday later, in the autumn.
WOMAN: Ah, I see. And where do you go?
BOY: We always go to the same place. It's called Cumbline.
WOMAN: Oh. Can you spell that for me, please?
BOY: Yes. It's C-U-M-B-L-I-N-E. It's a lovely place, with lakes and a forest.
WOMAN: Well, thank you, Ben. That's all.

[pause]

Now listen to Part 2 again.

[The recording is repeated.]

[pause]

That is the end of Part 2.

[pause]

Part 3 *Listen and look. There is one example.*

[pause]

Which photo did each person take?

[pause]

MAN: Would you like to look at these photographs? I go to a class every Monday evening with six other people. We have different jobs but we all want to be better photographers.

This picture of a storm at sea is beautiful, isn't it? Peter took it. He's a pilot and he knows a lot about the weather.

[pause]

Can you see the letter A? Now you listen and write a letter in each box.

[pause]

MAN: There's a businessman in the class. I don't know his name, but he takes some strange photos. This one is his – look. It's just a piece of pizza and some salad on a plate… it's not very interesting, is it?

[pause]

MAN: The best photographer in the class is Kim. She's a tennis player now, but she wants to work for a newspaper in the future. She took this picture of some camels by a pyramid. It's lovely, isn't it? She took it when she was on holiday.

[pause]

MAN: The photo of butterflies on a flower is Jane's. Do you like it? She studied medicine at university and now she's a doctor. Her pictures are always about the environment. She took this in her garden last year.

[pause]

MAN: I like this photo too. Katy's a policewoman and she took this picture when she was working at the airport one day. You can see a pilot. He's walking to his plane.

[pause]

MAN: And the last photo is Bill's – he's a car mechanic. His favourite hobby is space, you know, studying the moon and stars. Well, you can guess which one is his picture, can't you? Yes, of course, this one. It's called 'The sky at night'.

[pause]

Now listen to Part 3 again.

[The recording is repeated.]

[pause]

That is the end of Part 3.

[pause]

Part 4   *Listen and look. There is one example.*

[pause]

How did David go to town?

WOMAN: Did you go shopping in town yesterday, David?
BOY: Yes, we did, but we couldn't take the car.
WOMAN: Oh no. You've got a problem with it, haven't you? So, did you go by bus?
BOY: No. We took a taxi. It was much quicker.

[pause]

Can you see the tick? Now you listen and tick the box.

[pause]

1   *Which bowl did David buy?*

BOY: It's my grandmother's birthday next week. She's going to be 60.
WOMAN: Have you found a nice present for her?
BOY: Yes, I have. I bought her a fruit bowl.
WOMAN: Lovely! Is it made of glass?
BOY: No. I looked for a silver one, but they were too expensive. So I got this one. Look, it's made of wood.
WOMAN: Oh, it's very nice. She'll love that.

[pause]

2   *Which card will David choose?*

BOY: And I bought some cards. Which one shall I send to Grandmother for her birthday, Aunt Sue? The one with the snowman?

WOMAN: Mmm, I'm not sure, not for a birthday. I like these two cards, with rivers on them. One's got a bridge on it but I prefer the other one – the one with the boats.
BOY: Yes, I agree with you.

[pause]

3   *Where did David lose his umbrella?*

WOMAN: What's the matter, David? Is something wrong?
BOY: Yes, I've lost my umbrella. I took it with me yesterday when we went shopping.
WOMAN: Perhaps it's in the restaurant. You had lunch there with your mum, didn't you?
BOY: No, it's not there, I'm sure. But we went to the station to buy some tickets.
WOMAN: Let's telephone and ask.
BOY: Oh no. Now I remember. It's in the bookshop. I put it down when I was looking at a book and then I went outside without it.

[pause]

4   *Which are David's favourite biscuits?*

WOMAN: Did you buy anything else?
BOY: Yes, a box of my favourite biscuits. Can you remember my favourite ones?
WOMAN: Mmm… I forget… Have they got jam in them?
BOY: Well, I like them too, but no, these chocolate ones are my favourites.
WOMAN: Not coconut ones?
BOY: Ugh, no! They're horrible!

[pause]

5   *What time are they going to have dinner?*

BOY: Are you going to stay and have dinner with us, Aunt Sue?
WOMAN: Yes, I am. But I must leave before eight o'clock.
BOY: OK. Would you like to eat at half past six then?
WOMAN: That's too early for all of you, isn't it? Perhaps seven o'clock is better.
BOY: Yes. It is! We can watch the new animal programme on TV before dinner.

[pause]

Now listen to Part 4 again.

[The recording is repeated.]

[pause]

That is the end of Part 4.

[pause]

Part 5   *Listen and look at the picture. There is one example.*

[pause]

MAN: Would you like to help me finish this picture of my kitchen?
GIRL: Yes, I would, please.
MAN: OK. Well, first, can you see the boy's cup?

GIRL: Yes. It's next to his plate.
MAN: That's right. Please colour it red.

[pause]

Can you see the red cup next to the plate? This is an example. Now you listen and colour and draw and write.

[pause]

1

GIRL: So now, what shall I colour next?
MAN: Mmm… Let me think. Can you find the girl's plate?
GIRL: Oh yes – there it is. Now, what colour shall I use for that?
MAN: Mmm… What about blue?
GIRL: Right. That's a nice colour. Do you like it?
MAN: Yes. Very much.

[pause]

2

MAN: And now, can you see the window?
GIRL: Yes, of course.
MAN: Well, outside the window you can see three hills.
GIRL: Oh yes. Can I colour the smallest one, please?
MAN: Yes. Perhaps you can colour it purple?
GIRL: That's a strange colour!
MAN: Well, sometimes things look that colour when it's foggy.

[pause]

3

GIRL: Can I draw something now?
MAN: Of course. Can you see the bottle on the table?
GIRL: Yes, it's empty. I'd like to put a flower in it.
MAN: OK. You can draw one and colour it yellow.
GIRL: Right. I'll do that. There! That looks much nicer now.

[pause]

4

MAN: Would you like to write something now?
GIRL: OK. What can I write?
MAN: Well, can you see the picture on the wall? There are two swans in it.
GIRL: Yes. It's beautiful.
MAN: It's called 'The Lake'. Please write that word. Write it in the space at the bottom of the picture.

[pause]

5

MAN: And now, the last thing. The telephone. Can you see it?
GIRL: There are two, aren't there?
MAN: Oh yes, of course. Sorry, I meant the one on the shelf.
GIRL: OK. Right. I can see that one now. What colour shall I use?
MAN: Let me think. Would you like to colour it orange?

GIRL: No, I don't like that colour. Can I make it green?
MAN: Excellent! It looks very nice now.

[pause]

Now listen to Part 5 again.

[The recording is repeated.]

[pause]

That is the end of the Flyers Practice Listening Test 1.

Reading and Writing

Part 1 (10 marks)

1 a post office   2 a kangaroo   3 postcards
4 a camel   5 a cinema   6 an address
7 a library   8 a dolphin   9 newspapers
10 a museum

Part 2 (7 marks)

1 no   2 no   3 no   4 yes   5 yes   6 no
7 yes

Part 3 (5 marks)

1 B   2 A   3 C   4 B   5 A

Part 4 (6 marks)

1 chocolate   4 sky
2 burn   5 ate/had
3 dirty   6 John starts to enjoy camping

Part 5 (7 marks)

1 cows (and) sheep
2 (on) Saturday (and) Sunday (mornings)
3 (he/it had) (a) cough
4 she/it/the elephant was afraid
5 (to the) zoo hospital
6 (for) six/6 days
7 he/Harry helped him/it/the elephant

Part 6 (10 marks)

1 because   2 live   3 of   4 ago
5 be   6 them   7 no-one   8 which
9 any   10 study

Part 7 (5 marks)

1 hand   2 was/is   3 read
4 to   5 will/may/might/could/should

Speaking

Part	Examiner does this:	Examiner says this:	Minimum response expected from child:	Back-up questions:
	Usher brings candidate in.	Usher to examiner: **Hello, this is (child's name) *.** **Hello *, my name's** *Jane/ Ms Smith.*	**Hello**	
		What's your surname?	*Fernandez*	**What's your family name?**
		How old are you?	*eleven*	**Are you** *eleven*?
1	Shows candidate both **Find the difference** pictures. Points to the rocks in the water in each one.	**Now, here are two pictures. My picture is nearly the same as yours, but some things are different. For example, in my picture there are three rocks in the sea, but in your picture there are four. OK?**		
	Gives candidate his/her picture then describes things without pointing.	**I'm going to say something about my picture. You tell me how your picture is different.**		1. Point at relevant difference/s. 2. Repeat statement. 3. Ask back-up question.
		In my picture, two girls are playing volleyball. **In my picture, there's a shark on the right.** **In my picture, a woman's painting on the beach.** **In my picture, the man hasn't caught any fish.** **In my picture, I can see some clouds in the sky.** **In my picture, only one tree has coconuts.**	*In my picture, two girls are playing basketball.* *In my picture, there's a shark on the left.* *In my picture, the woman's taking a photo.* *In my picture, the man has caught a (big) fish.* *In my picture, I can see a rainbow/I can't see any clouds in the sky.* *In my picture, all the trees have coconuts.*	**Are the girls playing volleyball?** **Is the shark on the right?** **Is the woman painting?** **Has the man caught a fish?** **Can you see any clouds in the sky?** **How many trees have coconuts?**
2	Briefly shows candidate the **Information exchange** cards. Then gives candidate his/her card.	**Katy's and Richard's favourite toys are in these boxes. I don't know anything about Katy's favourite toy, but you do. So I'm going to ask you some questions.**		
	Points to the box on the left on candidate's card. Asks the questions.	**What is Katy's favourite toy?** **When did Katy get it?** **What's it made of?** **Why does Katy like it?** **Who gave it to her?**	*(a) camel* *five years ago* *(It's made of) wool.* *because it's very soft* *her aunt*	Point at the information if necessary.
	Points to the box on the right on the candidate's card.	**Now you don't know anything about Richard's favourite toy, so you ask me some questions.**		
	Responds using information on the examiner's card.	**a dinosaur** **It's made of plastic.** **six months ago** **his cousin** **because it's very ugly**	*What is Richard's favourite toy?* *What's it made of?* *When did Richard/he get it?* *Who gave it to him?* *Why does Richard/he like it?*	Point at information cues if necessary.

Part	Examiner does this:	Examiner says this:	Minimum response expected from child:	Back-up questions:
3	Shows candidate the **Tell the story** card. Allows time to look at it.	**These pictures tell a story. Just look at the pictures first.** **It's raining today, so Michael can't play outside. He isn't very happy. He's throwing and catching his ball in the living room.** **Now you tell the story.**		1. Point at the pictures. 2. Ask questions about the pictures.
			Now he hasn't caught the ball. It's hit a table. The ball has broken the table.	**Has Michael caught the ball?** **What has the ball hit?** **Is the table broken?**
			Michael is trying to glue the table together.	**What's Michael doing?**
			Now his mother has come into the room with a big cake. She's going to put the cake on the table. Michael is afraid.	**Who has come into the room?** **What's she carrying?** **Where's she going to put the cake?**
			The table has broken again. The cake is on the floor and Michael's mum isn't happy.	**Has the table broken again?** **Where's the cake?** **Is Michael's mum happy?**
4	Puts the pictures away and turns to the candidate.	**Now let's talk about your school.** **How many children are there in your class?** **Which lesson do you like best?** **What time does school start?** **What games do you play at school?** **Tell me about your best friend at school.**	*twenty* *history* *8.30* *table tennis* *His/her name's Juan/Maria.* *He's/she's very nice.* *He's/she's eleven.*	**Are there *twenty* children in your class?** **Do you like *history*?** **Does school start at *8.30*?** **Do you play *table tennis*?** **What's your best friend's name?** **Is he/she nice?** **How old is he/she?**
		OK, thank you, *. **Goodbye.**	*Goodbye.*	

* Remember to use the child's name throughout the test.

Test 2 Answers

Listening

Part 1 (5 marks)

Lines should be drawn between:

1 Sarah and the woman in the blue sweater, putting paper in the wastepaper bin
2 Betty and the woman picking up scissors from the floor
3 William and the man in the green shirt, at the computer
4 Harry and the man in the pink tie, standing and talking on the telephone
5 Helen and the smiling woman in the pink sweater, who is writing in a diary

Part 2 (5 marks)

1 half past eight/8.30/eight thirty/any of these answers plus a.m.
2 (a) (small) rucksack   3 (a) (plastic) plate
4 (a) torch   5 (a) towel

Part 3 (5 marks)

1 Journalist – H   2 Actress – F   3 Engineer – C
4 Footballer – E   5 Dentist – B

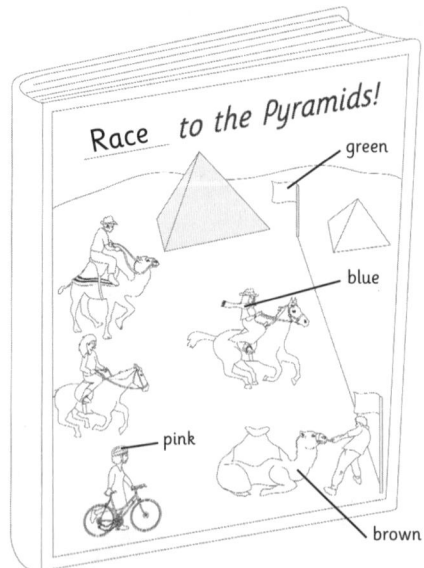

Part 4 (5 marks)

1 C   2 A   3 C   4 B   5 C

Part 5 (5 marks)

1 Colour the camel sitting on the ground – brown
2 Write the word 'Race' before 'to the Pyramids'
3 Draw a hat on the head of the woman pushing the bike, and colour the hat pink
4 Colour the flag between the two pyramids – green
5 Colour the scarf of the woman on the horse who is winning the race – blue

TRANSCRIPT   *Hello. This is the Cambridge Flyers Practice Listening Test, Test 2.*

Part 1   Listen and look. There is one example.

[pause]

BOY: It's interesting to see your office, Mum, but I don't know anyone here.
WOMAN: Oh, well. That's Richard over there, in the corner. He's drinking a cup of coffee.
BOY: Is he the man who's wearing a blue sweater?
WOMAN: Yes, that's him.

[pause]

Can you see the line? This is an example. Now you listen and draw lines.

[pause]

1

BOY: Who's that woman?
WOMAN: Where?
BOY: She's putting something in the bin.
WOMAN: Oh yes. That's Sarah. That looks better. I like a tidy office.

[pause]

2

WOMAN: And that's my friend Betty.
BOY: Where? What's she doing?
WOMAN: Her scissors have fallen on the floor and she's picking them up.
BOY: Oh yes. I can see her.

[pause]

3

WOMAN: That's William over there.
BOY: The man who's working on the computer?
WOMAN: Yes. The man in the green shirt.
BOY: His job looks interesting.

[pause]

4

BOY: Who's that talking on the telephone?
WOMAN: The man who's sitting down?
BOY: No, the one standing next to the desk.
WOMAN: Oh, that's Harry.

[pause]

5

WOMAN: Can you see the girl who's writing in her diary?
BOY: Yes. What's her name?
WOMAN: She's called Helen.
BOY: She looks very happy!
WOMAN: Yes, she is, because tomorrow is Saturday and she doesn't have to work!

[pause]

Now listen to Part 1 again.

[The recording is repeated.]

[pause]

That is the end of Part 1.

[pause]

Part 2 *Listen and look. There is one example.*

[pause]

WOMAN: Hello everyone. Please listen carefully, because I'm going to tell you some important things about our school camping trip to the lake this weekend. First, we are going to meet at Kirby Bridge. Write this in your books, please. That's K-I-R-B-Y. You all know that place, don't you?
BOY: Yes, Miss.

[pause]

Can you see the answer? Now you listen and write.

[pause]

WOMAN: Next, the time. Can we meet at half past eight?
BOY: Oh, that's very early!
WOMAN: No it isn't. You start school at that time every day!
BOY: OK. What do we have to take with us, Miss?
WOMAN: Well, we'll only be there for two days, so don't bring a heavy suitcase! But you will need a small rucksack.
BOY: My brother's got one. I can use his. Shall we bring some food with us?
WOMAN: No, you don't need any because we can

buy some at the shop in the village. But please bring a plastic plate with you.
BOY: OK. What about a torch, Miss?
WOMAN: Yes. That's very important because there aren't any lights in our tents! Now what else? I know. The farmer is going to let us use the showers at the farm. Isn't that kind? So, you will all need to bring a towel with you.
BOY: Right. Is that everything?
WOMAN: Yes. So, see you all tomorrow.
BOY: OK. Bye, Miss.

[pause]

Now listen to Part 2 again.

[The recording is repeated.]

[pause]

That is the end of Part 2.

[pause]

Part 3 *Listen and look. There is one example.*

[pause]

All the people in Emma's family go to work in different ways. How does each person go to work?

[pause]

WOMAN: My aunt is a nurse at the hospital in town. It isn't far from her house so she goes to work by bicycle.

[pause]

Can you see the letter D? Now you listen and write a letter in each box.

[pause]

WOMAN: My cousin is a footballer. He plays for a famous team. He's very rich and he's just bought a helicopter. He loves flying and he uses it to go to all his matches.

[pause]

WOMAN: My brother is an engineer. He lives on an island, so he has to go to work by boat every day.

[pause]

WOMAN: My uncle is a journalist. He writes for a newspaper and he uses his motorbike to go to work. There's always a lot of traffic in the city, so it's better than a car.

[pause]

WOMAN: My sister has a very good job. She's a dentist. She takes a train to go to work. There is a bus, but it's very slow.

[pause]

WOMAN: And last, my other cousin is an actress and she works at different theatres. When she goes to work, she prefers to take a taxi because it's quick and easy.

[pause]

Now listen to Part 3 again.

[The recording is repeated.]

[pause]

That is the end of Part 3.

[pause]

Part 4 *Listen and look. There is one example.*

[pause]

Which is Katy's new house?

MAN: Hello, Katy. Did you have a nice weekend in your new house?
GIRL: Yes thanks, Mr Brown. It's got a great garden, with some big trees for me to climb.
MAN: Oh! What else has it got?
GIRL: It's got a lovely balcony too.

[pause]

Can you see the tick? Now you listen and tick the box.

[pause]

1 *Where is Katy's new house?*

MAN: Is your new house in the town, near our school, Katy?
GIRL: No, it's in the countryside.
MAN: In a village?
GIRL: No. There aren't any other houses near us.

[pause]

2 *What's Katy's new bedroom like?*

GIRL: My new bedroom is very nice. I've got a desk in it. I can do my homework there.
MAN: Have you got a television too?
GIRL: No, but I've got a CD player. I love listening to music.
MAN: That sounds nice.

[pause]

3 *What does Katy's dad do?*

GIRL: My dad works at home now.
MAN: Oh. Is he a businessman?
GIRL: No, he's a photographer. He takes pictures for magazines.
MAN: Oh. That's an interesting job!

[pause]

4 *What is Katy going to have for supper?*

GIRL: I'm going to make supper tonight.
MAN: Oh! What are you going to make? Can you make pizza? Or soup?
GIRL: No, I can't make those things. I'm going to make a salad.
MAN: Lovely!

[pause]

5 *What time is Katy's mum going to come home tonight?*

MAN: Where does your mum work, Katy?
GIRL: She works in a shop. She usually comes home at five o'clock but tonight she's going to be late.
MAN: Why is that?
GIRL: On Thursdays the shop closes at six o'clock, so she gets home at half past six.

[pause]

Now listen to Part 4 again.

[The recording is repeated.]

[pause]

That is the end of Part 4.

[pause]

Part 5 *Listen and look at the picture. There is one example.*

[pause]

MAN: Would you like to colour this picture of a book?
GIRL: Yes please. What's it about?
MAN: It's about some people who are trying to win some money in a competition. The first person who arrives at the pyramids wins.
GIRL: Oh! Can I colour the biggest pyramid?
MAN: Yes. You can colour it yellow.

[pause]

Can you see the yellow pyramid? This is an example. Now you listen and colour and write and draw.

[pause]

1

MAN: Can you see the camel on the right?
GIRL: The one that's lying down?
MAN: Yes.
GIRL: It looks very tired. Shall I colour it?
MAN: Yes. Colour it brown.

[pause]

2

MAN: Would you like to write something?
GIRL: Excellent!
MAN: Can you see the name of the book?
GIRL: Mmm. There's a word missing.
MAN: The book is called 'Race to the Pyramids!' Write the missing word, please.

[pause]

3

MAN: And now for some drawing. Can you see the woman with the bike?

GIRL: Yes. What's she doing?
MAN: It's broken and she's pushing it.
GIRL: She looks hot. Shall I draw a hat on her head?
MAN: Yes, and then colour it pink.

[pause]

4

MAN: Now, can you see the flag?
GIRL: The one next to the camel?
MAN: No, the one between the pyramids.
GIRL: OK.
MAN: Colour it green.

[pause]

5

MAN: Last, I want you to find the woman who's riding a horse.
GIRL: I can see her. She's wearing a long dress.
MAN: That's right. Can you see her scarf?
GIRL: Yes.
MAN: Well, colour it blue.
GIRL: Great. She's winning the race, I think!

[pause]

Now listen to Part 5 again.

[The recording is repeated.]

[pause]

That is the end of the Flyers Practice Listening Test 2.

Reading and Writing

Part 1 (10 marks)

1 butterflies   2 the sky   3 Geography
4 swans   5 museums   6 stations
7 ice   8 dinosaurs   9 Maths
10 a storm

Part 2 (7 marks)

1 yes   2 no   3 no   4 yes   5 yes
6 yes   7 no

Part 3 (5 marks)

1 B   2 C   3 C   4 A   5 B

Part 4 (6 marks)

1 eyes
2 pulled
3 ate/had
4 park
5 sunny
6 The day we made snowmen

Part 5 (7 marks)

1 hot and tired
2 old and small
3 (a) lizard
4 (because) he/David was thirsty
5 (from) (a) tree
6 (his/David's) dad/father
7 William

Part 6 (10 marks)

1 who   2 ago   3 later   4 fly
5 with   6 can   7 This   8 a
9 but   10 will

Part 7 (5 marks)

1 read   2 on   3 opened
4 at   5 you

Speaking

Part	Examiner does this:	Examiner says this:	Minimum response expected from child:	Back-up questions:
	Usher brings candidate in.	Usher to examiner: **Hello, this is (child's name) *.** Hello *, my name's *Jane/ Ms Smith.*	*Hello*	
		What's your surname?	*Fernandez*	**What's your family name?**
		How old are you?	*eleven*	**Are you** *eleven***?**
1	Shows candidate both **Find the difference** pictures. Points to the spoons in each one. Gives candidate his/her picture then describes things without pointing.	**Now, here are two pictures. My picture is nearly the same as yours, but some things are different. For example, the spoons in my picture are blue, but in your picture they're yellow.** **I'm going to say something about my picture. You tell me how your picture is different.** **In my picture, there's a lamp on the red table.** **In my picture, you can see some forks and knives on the green table.** **In my picture, the window is open.** **In my picture, the old man is sitting down.** **In my picture, the girls have got long hair.** **In my picture, you can see the moon.**	*In my picture, there's a plant.* *In my picture, you can't see any forks or knives.* *In my picture, the window is closed.* *In my picture, the old man is standing.* *In my picture, the girls have got short hair.* *In my picture, you can see the sun.*	1. Point at relevant difference/s. 2. Repeat statement. 3. Ask back-up question. **What's on the red table?** **Can you see any forks or knives on the green table?** **Is the window open?** **Is the old man sitting down?** **Have the girls got long hair?** **Can you see the moon?**
2	Briefly shows candidate the **Information exchange** cards. Then gives candidate his/her card. Points to the man on the left on candidate's card. Asks the questions.	**David and Emma are friends. Their fathers are friends, too. I don't know anything about David's father, but you do. So I'm going to ask you some questions.** **How old is David's father?** **Where does he work?** **What's his job?** **Which sport does he play?** **What time does he come home?**	*(He's) 35.* *at the university* *(He's a) teacher.* *football* *(at) 7 o'clock*	Point at the information if necessary.
	Points to the man on the right on the candidate's card. Responds using information on the examiner's card.	**Now, you don't know anything about Emma's father, so you ask me some questions.** He's 39. He's a doctor. at the hospital at 7.30 tennis	*How old is he?* *What's his job?* *Where does he work?* *What time does he come home?* *What sport does he play?*	Point at information cues if necessary.

Part	Examiner does this:	Examiner says this:	Minimum response expected from child:	Back-up questions:
3	Shows candidate the **Tell the story** card. Allows time to look at it.	**These pictures tell a story. Just look at the pictures first.** **John and his sister Sally are walking in the forest. They're going to have a picnic in the field across the river.** **Now you tell the story.**		1. Point at the pictures. 2. Ask questions about the pictures.
			They are at the bridge over the river. John has crossed the bridge, but Sally can't cross because the bridge has broken.	**Has John crossed the bridge?** **Can Sally cross too?** **Why not?**
			Sally is by the river. She is taking off her shoes. She wants to walk across the river.	**What is Sally doing?** **What does she want to do?**
			John is saying, 'Don't go in the water!' He can see a crocodile in the water.	**What is John saying?** **What can he see in the water?**
			Sally is on the back of the crocodile. The crocodile is swimming across the river. John is going to give the crocodile some food.	**Where's Sally?** **Where's the crocodile going?** **What's John going to give the crocodile?**
4	Puts the pictures away and turns to the candidate.	**Now let's talk about what you do in the evening.** **Where do you do your homework?**	*in my bedroom*	**Do you do your homework *in your bedroom*?**
		What do you have for dinner?	*chicken and rice*	**Do you have *chicken and rice* for dinner?**
		What do you do after dinner?	*I watch TV.*	**Do you *watch TV*?**
		What time do you go to bed?	*nine o'clock*	**Do you go to bed at *nine o'clock*?**
		Tell me about your bedroom.	*It's big.* *The walls are pink.*	**Is your bedroom big?** **What colour are the walls?**
			There's a computer.	**Is there a *computer* in your bedroom?**
		OK, thank you, *. **Goodbye.**	*Goodbye.*	

* Remember to use the child's name throughout the test.

Test 3 Answers

Listening

Part 1 (5 marks)

Lines should be drawn between:
1 Helen and the girl in the red T-shirt holding a boat
2 David and the boy in the water who is shouting
3 Emma and the girl shivering in the pink towel
4 Michael and the boy in red shorts throwing a ball.
5 Katy and the girl with short hair on the towel eating biscuits

Part 2 (5 marks)

1 (of) January   2 Salford (correct spelling)   3 Tuesday(s)
4 (the) 22(nd)/twenty-second   5 plants

Part 3 (5 marks)

1 Torch – F   2 Umbrella – H   3 Diary – B   4 Hairbrush – D
5 Chocolate – E

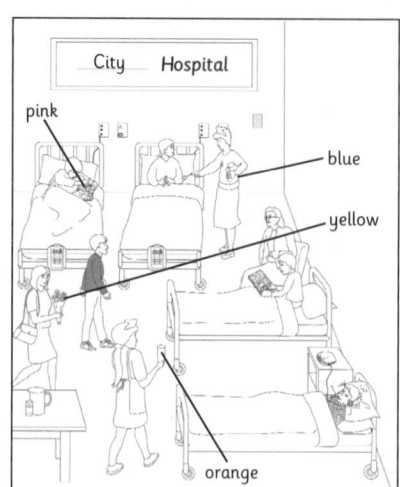

Part 4 (5 marks)

1 B   2 B   3 A   4 B   5 C

Part 5 (5 marks)

1 Colour comic being read by boy lying down in bed – pink
2 Colour uniform of nurse giving medicine to boy on spoon – blue
3 Draw flowers in hand of woman visitor walking across room and
  colour them yellow.
4 Write 'City' before 'Hospital'
5 Colour juice in glass carried by nurse walking across room – orange

TRANSCRIPT   *Hello. This is the Cambridge Flyers*
              Practice Listening Test, Test 3.

   Part 1   Listen and look. There is one example.

              [pause]

MAN: There are a lot of people at the lake today!
GIRL: Yes, it's very hot, isn't it?
MAN: Who are they all?
GIRL: Well, the boy who's swimming is Richard.

       [pause]

       Can you see the line? This is an
       example. Now you listen and
       draw lines.

       [pause]

   1

MAN: Which girl is Helen? Is she here?
GIRL: She's over there, on the left.
MAN: What's she doing?

GIRL: She's going to sail her boat.
MAN: Oh yes. I can see her now. She hasn't put
       it in the water yet.

       [pause]

   2

MAN: Who's that boy near the rocks?
GIRL: Which one?
MAN: He's just jumped into the water.
GIRL: Oh, that's David. The boy who's shouting!

       [pause]

   3

GIRL: Look at Emma! She's the girl who's
       standing by the lake.
MAN: The girl with the towel?
GIRL: Yes. She's just come out of the water.
MAN: Her hair's all wet.

       [pause]

   4

GIRL: That's Michael over there.

MAN: Which boy is he?
GIRL: The boy who's throwing a ball.
MAN: Oh yes, the tall boy. I like his red shorts.

[pause]

5

MAN: Is Katy here too?
GIRL: Yes, she's over there, sitting on a towel.
MAN: The girl with long hair?
GIRL: No, she's got short hair.
MAN: I can see her. She's eating some biscuits.

[pause]

Now listen to Part 1 again.

[The recording is repeated.]

That is the end of Part 1.

[pause]

Part 2 *Listen and look. There is one example.*

[pause]

GIRL: Hello. I'd like to come to your art club, please.
MAN: OK. Let's see. Can I ask you some questions? First, what's your name?
GIRL: Ann Knight.
MAN: How do you spell your surname?
GIRL: K-N-I-G-H-T.
MAN: Thank you.

[pause]

Can you see the answer? Now you listen and write.

[pause]

MAN: Now, Ann, how old are you?
GIRL: I'm 12. My birthday is the fifteenth of January.
MAN: Right. OK. And where do you live, Ann?
GIRL: At 26 Salford Street.
MAN: Is that S-U-L-F-O-R-D?
GIRL: No, S-A-L-F-O-R-D.
MAN: Thank you. Next question! Which day would you like to come to the club? We meet every day after school.
GIRL: Um, I can only come on Tuesday. Is that OK?
MAN: That's fine.
GIRL: Can I ask you a question?
MAN: Of course you can.
GIRL: I can't come next week. Can I start the week after that?
MAN: Of course you can. That's April the twenty-second. Don't forget!
GIRL: OK. Thanks.
MAN: My last question. What kind of things do you like painting? Animals? People?
GIRL: They're OK, but I like painting plants and trees best.
MAN: Right. You'll enjoy our club, I'm sure!

[pause]

Now listen to Part 2 again.

[The recording is repeated.]

[pause]

That is the end of Part 2.

[pause]

Part 3 *Listen and look. There is one example.*

[pause]

May has gone camping and has left all these things at home. Where are they?

[pause]

WOMAN: When I go camping I always forget to take something. I can't find my soap and I want to wash my hands. Where is it? Oh, no! I've left it in the shower at home!

[pause]

Can you see the letter G? Now you listen and write a letter in each box.

[pause]

WOMAN: Now I want to brush my hair and I can't find my brush! It's still by the mirror in my bedroom!

[pause]

WOMAN: It's started raining and I haven't got my umbrella. I remember now, I used it when I went shopping. It was too wet to put on the balcony so I put it in the bath.

[pause]

WOMAN: It's very dark now and I need my torch. I can't find it anywhere. Now I remember! It's at home. I used it last week and then... I put it on top of the fridge. I must buy one.

[pause]

WOMAN: Now, where's my diary? I want to write something in it. Oh no, I was writing in it last week when someone phoned. I left it on the kitchen table and forgot to bring it with me.

[pause]

WOMAN: I'm cold and hungry. I know, I'll have some chocolate. Oh no. It's in the kitchen, too. I've left it next to the cooker!

[pause]

Now listen to Part 3 again.

[The recording is repeated.]

[pause]

That is the end of Part 3.

[pause]

Part 4 *Listen and look. There is one example.*

[pause]

What did William do in the school holidays?

MAN: Hello, William. Did you enjoy the holidays?
BOY: Yes thanks. We went to London for a few days.
MAN: Did you visit any museums or theatres?
BOY: No, but we went to the circus. It was excellent.

[pause]

Can you see the tick? Now you listen and tick the box.

[pause]

1 *Who did William go with?*

MAN: Did you go with your mum and dad, William?
BOY: Yes.
MAN: What about your brother and sister?
BOY: My brother came but my sister didn't.

[pause]

2 *Where did William stay?*

MAN: What was your hotel like?
BOY: Very nice. It was near a lovely park.
MAN: Oh. Was it a big new hotel?
BOY: No. It was small.

[pause]

3 *What did William have for breakfast?*

BOY: The breakfast in the hotel was excellent.
MAN: What could you have?
BOY: Oh, everything. There was coffee, cheese, fish, meat, bread, cakes…
MAN: So, what did you choose?
BOY: I had bread and jam and a glass of milk every morning.

[pause]

4 *What did William buy?*

BOY: We went shopping one day.
MAN: Oh. Did you buy those gloves?
BOY: No, they were a Christmas present.
MAN: Did you buy anything?
BOY: Yes. I got a new football. I saw a great rucksack, but it was too expensive.

[pause]

5 *Which film did William see?*

BOY: We went to see a film one night.
MAN: Did you? Did you see 'Lost at Sea'?
BOY: No, we wanted to go to 'Coconut Island', but the cinema was full.
MAN: So what did you see?
BOY: We saw 'The Blue Whale'. It was good!

[pause]

Now listen to Part 4 again.

[The recording is repeated.]

[pause]

That is the end of Part 4.

[pause]

Part 5 *Listen and look at the picture. There is one example.*

[pause]

BOY: Oh, look! It's a picture of a hospital. Can I colour it?
WOMAN: Of course you can.
BOY: What shall I do first?
WOMAN: Can you see the boy who's visiting someone?
BOY: Yes. Shall I colour his sweater?
WOMAN: OK. Colour it green.

[pause]

Can you see the boy's green sweater? This is an example. Now you listen and colour and draw and write.

[pause]

1

WOMAN: Look at the boy who's lying in bed.
BOY: The boy on the left of the picture?
WOMAN: Yes.
BOY: He's looking at a comic.
WOMAN: Well, please colour it pink.
BOY: OK.

[pause]

2

WOMAN: Next, I want you to find the nurse who's giving a boy some medicine.
BOY: I can see her. She's got short hair.
WOMAN: That's right. Can you colour her uniform, please?
BOY: Yes. I'm going to colour it blue.

[pause]

3

WOMAN: Now for some drawing.
BOY: Excellent.
WOMAN: Find the woman who's visiting someone. She's walking across the room. Draw some flowers in her hand.
BOY: Right. I've done that. Can I colour them red?
WOMAN: No, colour them yellow.

[pause]

4

WOMAN: Would you like to write something now?
BOY: Yes please.
WOMAN: Can you see the word 'Hospital'?
BOY: Yes.
WOMAN: Well, write the name 'City' next to it.

[pause]

5

BOY:	Can I colour something else, please?
WOMAN:	OK. Find the glass.
BOY:	The one on the table?
WOMAN:	No. The one in the nurse's hand. Let's put some juice in it. Colour it orange.
BOY:	OK. That's nice!

[pause]

Now listen to Part 5 again.

[The recording is repeated.]

[pause]

That is the end of the Flyers Practice Listening Test 3.

Reading and Writing

Part 1 (10 marks)

1 a playground   2 a station   3 traffic
4 secretaries   5 an ambulance   6 a rainbow
7 a map   8 an umbrella   9 clowns
10 nurses

Part 2 (7 marks)

1 yes   2 yes   3 no   4 yes   5 yes
6 no   7 yes

Part 3 (5 marks)

1 A   2 A   3 C   4 B   5 B

Part 4 (6 marks)

1 swings
2 bird
3 pocket
4 cried
5 ran
6 Helen loses her key

Part 5 (7 marks)

1 (the) Pyramids
2 the/a (beautiful) boat
3 (to) ride (on) a camel (too)
4 a/the zoo
5 take a/(Betty's) photo (of Betty/her);
   (she) took a/Betty's/her photo
6 happy
7 (because) he was afraid/scared/frightened

Part 6 (10 marks)

1 for   2 was   3 had   4 moving
5 all   6 have   7 them   8 when
9 don't   10 on

Part 7 (5 marks)

1 in
2 plane/an aeroplane/an aircraft
3 to
4 them
5 close/shut/carry/lift

Speaking

Part	Examiner does this:	Examiner says this:	Minimum response expected from child:	Back-up questions:
	Usher brings candidate in.	Usher to examiner: **Hello, this is (child's name) *.** **Hello *, my name's** *Jane/ Ms Smith.*	*Hello*	
		What's your surname?	*Fernandez*	**What's your family name?**
		How old are you?	*eleven*	**Are you** *ten***?**
1	Shows candidate both **Find the difference** pictures. Points to the parrots in the tent in each one.	**Now, here are two pictures. My picture is nearly the same as yours, but some things are different. For example, there are two parrots in my picture, but in your picture there are three. OK?**		
	Gives candidate his/her picture then describes things without pointing.	**I'm going to say something about my picture. You tell me how your picture is different.**		1. Point at relevant difference/s. 2. Repeat statement. 3. Ask back-up question.
		In my picture, the horse's hat is red. **In my picture, the box is on the left.** **In my picture, the big clown has got an umbrella in his hand.** **In my picture, a man is taking a photo.** **In my picture, there are two chairs behind the big clown.** **In my picture, you can see the moon in the sky.**	*In my picture, the horse's hat is blue.* *In my picture, the box is on the right.* *In my picture, the big clown has got a guitar in his hand.* *In my picture, a woman is taking a photo.* *In my picture, there's one chair behind the big clown.* *In my picture, you can't see the moon/you can see stars in the sky.*	**What colour is the horse's hat?** **Is the box on the left?** **Has the big clown got an umbrella in his hand?** **Who's taking a photo?** **How many chairs are there behind the big clown?** **What can you see in the sky?**
2	Briefly shows candidate the **Information exchange** cards. Then gives candidate his/her card. Points to the boy's box on candidate's card.	**This is David and Betty. They are taking their pets to school. I don't know anything about David's pet, but you do. So I'm going to ask you some questions.**		
	Asks the questions.	**What pet has David got?** **What colour is it?** **What does it eat?** **How old is it?** **What's the pet's name?**	*(a) rabbit* *(It's) white.* *(It eats) carrots.* *(It's) four months old.* *Peter*	Point at the information if necessary.
	Points to the girl's box on the candidate's card.	**Now, you don't know anything about Betty's pet, so you ask me some questions.**		
	Responds using information on the examiner's card.	**a spider** **Sarah** **black** **six weeks old** **flies**	*What pet has Betty got?* *What's the pet's/its name?* *What colour is it?* *How old is it?* *What does it eat?*	Point at information cues if necessary.

Part	Examiner does this:	Examiner says this:	Minimum response expected from child:	Back-up questions:
3	Shows candidate the **Tell the story** card. Allows time to look at it.	**These pictures tell a story. Just look at the pictures first.** **Emma and Jill are in their bedroom with their mother. She isn't happy because the room is untidy. She is saying, 'It's half past six. You must tidy your room and then you can watch TV in bed.'** **Now you tell the story.**		1. Point at the pictures. 2. Ask questions about the pictures.
			Now Emma and Jill are tidying the room. They're putting the toys in the cupboard.	**Are they tidying the room now?** **Where are they putting the toys?**
			The room is tidy now. It's nine o'clock and Emma and Jill are in bed. They're watching TV.	**Is the room tidy now?** **Where are the children now?** **What are they doing?**
			It's midnight. The toys are coming out of the cupboard and playing together.	**What time is it now?** **What's happening?**
			It's the next morning. Their mother has come into the room to wake the girls up. The room is untidy again. She's thinking, 'What has happened here?'	**Who's coming into the room?** **Is the room still tidy?** **What's the mother thinking?**
4	Puts the pictures away and turns to the candidate.	**Now let's talk about your weekends.** **What do you do on Saturday** morning?** **Where do you go on Saturday** morning?** **What time do you get up on Sunday** morning?** **What do you eat for lunch on Sunday**?** **Tell me about other things you do at the weekend.**	*I go shopping.* *to the park* *ten o'clock* *chicken* *I sometimes go to the beach.* *I play football with my friends.* *I go to the cinema.*	**Do you go *shopping*?** **Do you go to the *park*?** **Do you get up late?** **Do you have *chicken*?** **Do you go to the *beach*?** **Do you play *football*?** **Do you go to the *cinema*?**
		OK, thank you, *. **Goodbye.**	*Goodbye.*	

* Remember to use the child's name throughout the test.
** Use an appropriate weekend day.

COMBINED STARTERS, MOVERS AND FLYERS THEMATIC VOCABULARY LIST

For ease of reference, vocabulary is arranged in semantic groups or themes. Some words appear under more than one heading.

In addition to the topics, notions and concepts listed for the syllabus, the following categories appear:
- miscellaneous objects/nouns
- adjectives
- determiners
- adverbs
- prepositions
- pronouns
- conjunctions
- verbs

s – first appears at *Starters*

m – first appears at *Movers*

f – first appears at *Flyers*

ANIMALS

s animal
m bat
m bear
s bird
f butterfly
f camel
s cat
s chicken
s cow
s crocodile
f dinosaur
s dog
m dolphin
s duck
s elephant
s fish (s & pl)
m fly
s frog
s giraffe
s goat
s hippo
s horse
f insect
m kangaroo
m lion
s lizard

s monkey
s mouse/mice
f octopus
m panda
m parrot
m pet
m rabbit
m shark
s sheep (s & pl)
s snake
s spider
f swan
s tiger
m whale

THE BODY AND THE FACE

s arm
m back
m beard
m blonde
s body
m curly
s ear
s eye
s face
m fair
s foot/feet

s hair
s hand
s head
s leg
m moustache
s mouth
m neck
s nose
m shoulder
m stomach
m straight
m tooth/teeth

CLOTHES

f belt
s clothes
m coat
s dress
s glasses
f glove
s handbag
s hat
s jacket
s jeans
f pocket
m scarf
s shirt

s shoe
f shorts
s skirt
s sock
m sweater
s T-shirt
f tights
s trousers
f uniform
s wear

FAMILY, FRIENDS AND OURSELVES

s Ann
m aunt
s baby
s Ben
f Betty
s Bill
s birthday
s boy
s brother
s child/children
m cousin
s dad(dy)
m Daisy
m daughter
f David
f Emma
s family
s father
m Fred
s friend
s girl
m granddaughter
s grandfather
s grandmother
m grandparent
m grandson
f Harry
s he
f Helen
s her
s him
s his
f husband
s I
m Jane
m Jill
m Jim
m John
f Katy
s Kim
s live
s man/men
f married

m Mary
s May
s me
f Michael
s Miss
s mother
s Mr
s Mrs
s mum(my)
s my
s name
s Nick
s old
m parent
s Pat
m Paul
m person/people
m Peter
f Richard
m Sally
s Sam
f Sarah
s she
s sister
m son
s Sue
f surname
s their
s them
s they
s Tom
m uncle
s us
s we
f wife
f William
s woman/women
s you
s young
s your

FOLKLORE AND FANTASY

f castle
f cave
f future
f planet
f secret
f space
f strange
f wish

FOOD AND DRINK

s apple
s banana
s bean

f biscuit
s bread
s breakfast
s burger
f butter
s cake
s carrot
m cheese
s chicken
f chocolate
f chopsticks
s coconut
m coffee
f dinner
s drink (n & v)
s eat
s egg
s fish
f flour
s food
f fork
s French fries
m fruit
s ice cream
f jam
s juice
f knife
s lemon
s lemonade
s lime
s lunch
s mango
f meal
s meat
s milk
s onion
s orange
m pasta
s pea
s pear
f pepper
m picnic
s pineapple
f pizza
f plate
s potato
s rice
f salad
f salt
m sandwich
s sausage
f snack
m soup
f spoon
f sugar
s supper

f sweet
m tea
s tomato
f vegetable
s water
s watermelon

HEALTH

f chemist (chemist's)
m cold
m cough
f dentist
f doctor
m earache
m fine
m headache
f hospital
m hurt
f ill
m matter (What's the matter?)
f medicine
f nurse
m stomach-ache
m temperature
m toothache

THE HOME

m address
m apartment
s armchair
m balcony
m basement
s bath
s bathroom
s bed
s bedroom
s bookcase
s box
s camera
s chair
s clock
f cooker
s cupboard
s dining room
s doll
s door
m downstairs
m flat
m floor
s flower
f fridge
s garden
s hall
m home
s house
s kitchen

s lamp
m lift (USA elevator)
s living room
s mat
s mirror
s phone
s radio
s room
f shelf
m shower
s sleep
s sofa
m stairs
s table
f telephone
s television/TV
f toilet
s toy
s tree
m upstairs
s watch
s window

OCCUPATIONS AND THE WORLD OF WORK

f actor/actress
f airport
f ambulance
f artist
f business
f businessman/woman
f circus
m clown
f cook
f dentist
f doctor
f engineer
f factory
f farmer
f fireman/woman
f footballer
m hospital
f job
f journalist
f mechanic
f meeting
f news
f newspaper
f nurse
f office
f painter
f photographer
f pilot
m pirate
f policeman/woman
f police station

f secretary
f singer
f tennis player
m work

PLACES AND DIRECTIONS

f airport
m bank
f bookshop
f bridge
m bus station
f bus stop
m café
f chemist('s)
m cinema
f circus
f club
f college
f corner
f end
m farm
f fire station
f front
f get to
m hospital
f kilometres
f left
m library
f London
m market
f museum
f over
m park
m playground
f police station
f post office
f restaurant
f right
m road
m shop
f station
f straight on
s street
m supermarket
m swimming pool
f theatre
f way
m zoo

SCHOOL AND THE CLASSROOM, AND LANGUAGE AND TESTS

s alphabet
s answer
f Art

s ask
f bin
s board
s book
s bookcase
s class
s classroom
s close
f club
f college
s colour
s colour (in)
f competition
s correct
s cross
s desk
f dictionary
s draw
s English
s eraser
f exam (examination)
s example
s find
s floor
f Geography
f glue
f group
f history
m homework
s know (don't know)
f language
s learn
s lesson
s letter (as in alphabet)
s line
s listen (to)
s look
f Maths
m mistake
s no
s number
s open
s page
s part
s pen
s pencil
s picture
m playground
s question
s read
s right (correct)
s ruler
s school
f Science
f scissors

s sentence
f shelf
f student
f subject
s teacher
s tell
s test
m text
s tick
s understand
f university
s wall
s word
s write
s yes

SPORTS AND LEISURE-TIME ACTIVITIES

s badminton
s ball
s baseball
s basketball
s beach
s book
s bounce
s camera
m CD
m comic/comic book
f diary
s doll
s draw(ing)
f drum
s enjoy
s favourite
m film
s fish(ing)
s football
s game
f golf
s guitar
s hit
s hobby
s hockey
m holiday
f hotel
s kick v
m kick n
s kite
s listen (to)
m music
s paint(ing)
m party
s photo
s piano
s picture

s play (with)
f player (CD player)
f programme
f pyramid
f race
s radio
s read
f rucksack
s run
s sing
m skate
f sledge
f snowball
f snowman
s soccer
s song
s sport
s story
f suitcase
s swim
s table tennis
f team
s television/TV
s tennis
f tent
f torch
s toy
m video
f volleyball
s watch

TRANSPORT

f ambulance
f bicycle
s bike
s boat
s bus
s car
s fly
s go
s helicopter
s lorry
s motorbike
s plane
s ride
s run
s swim
f taxi
f traffic
s train
s walk

WEATHER

m cloud
m cloudy

f fog
f foggy
f ice
m rain
m rainbow
f sky
m snow
f storm
s sun
m sunny
m weather
m wind
m windy

THE WORLD AROUND US

f air
f bridge
f cave
m city
m country(side)
f environment
m field
f fire
m forest
m grass
m ground
f hill
m island
m jungle
m lake
m leaf/leaves
m moon
m mountain
m plant
m river
m road
m rock
s sea
f sky
f space
m star
s street
m town
m village
m waterfall
m world

COLOURS

s black
s blue
s brown
f gold
s green
s grey (or gray)
s orange

s pink
s purple
s red
f silver
f spot
f stripe
s white
s yellow

LOCATION AND POSITION

s at
s behind
s between
s here
s in
s in front of
s next to
s on
s there
s under

MISCELLANEOUS OBJECTS AND OTHER NOUNS

m age
s bag
m blanket
m bottom
s box
f brush
f card (birthday)
f comb
s computer
s day
m difference
f envelope
m fan
f flag
f key
m kind (type)
f letter (send a letter)
f light(s)
f magazine
m map
f money
s monster
f newspaper
s night
f paper
m place
f postcard
f present
f problem
f queen
s robot
f secret

f soap
f stamp
f swing
f tape recorder
f telephone
m thing
m toothbrush
m top
f torch
m towel
m treasure
f umbrella
m wash

NUMBERS

s Cardinals: 1–10
m Cardinals: 11–20
f Cardinals: 21–1000
m Ordinals: 1st–10th
f Ordinals: 11th–31st
f zero

CONTAINERS

m bottle (of)
m bowl (of)
m cup (of)
m glass (of)

QUANTITY AND MEASURING

f a few
f a little
f a piece of
f enough
f few
f half
f many
f much
f quarter

THE SENSES

f feel like
f look like
f smell like
f sound like
f taste like

MATERIALS

f card
f glass
f gold
f metal
f paper
f plastic

f   silver
f   wood
f   wool

TIME EXPRESSIONS

f   a.m.
m   after
s   afternoon
f   ago
m   always
m   before
f   century
f   date
f   early
s   end
m   evening
m   every
f   future
f   half
f   hour
f   late
f   later
f   midday
f   midnight
f   minute
f   month
m   morning
m   never
f   o'clock
f   p.m.
f   past
f   quarter
m   sometimes
f   time
s   today
f   tomorrow
f   tonight
m   week
m   weekend
f   year
m   yesterday
    The days of the week:
m   Monday
m   Tuesday
m   Wednesday
m   Thursday
m   Friday
m   Saturday
m   Sunday

THE YEAR

f   January
f   February
f   March
f   April

f   May
f   June
f   July
f   August
f   September
f   October
f   November
f   December
f   Christmas
f   Easter
f   spring
f   summer
f   autumn
f   winter
f   year

GREETINGS AND OTHER FORMULAIC EXPRESSIONS

m   all right
s   bye(-bye)
f   excellent!
m   excuse me!
m   good morning/afternoon/evening
    /night
s   goodbye
m   great!
s   happy birthday!
s   hello
s   here you are
m   How about? (suggestion)
m   I didn't understand/hear you
s   I don't know
s   no
f   of course (not)!
s   oh
s   OK
s   Pardon?
s   please
s   right
s   so
s   so do I
s   sorry
s   thank you
s   thanks
s   then
s   well
m   What about...?
m   What did you say?
m   What's the matter?
s   yes

ADJECTIVES

m   afraid
m   all
m   any

m   bad
s   beautiful
m   best
m   better
s   big
f   boring
f   broken
m   careful
f   cheap
s   clean
f   clever
f   closed
m   cloudy
m   cold
f   dangerous
f   dark
f   dear
m   different
m   difficult
s   dirty
s   double
f   dry
f   each
f   early
m   easy
f   empty
f   enough
s   English
m   every
f   excellent
f   expensive
f   extinct
m   famous
f   fast
m   fat
s   favourite
t   few
m   fine
f   friendly
f   full (of)
f   gold
s   good
s   happy
f   hard
f   heavy
f   high
f   horrible
m   hot
m   hungry
f   ill
f   important
f   interesting
f   kind
m   last
f   late

f left (direction)
f light
f little
s long
m loud
f lovely
f low
f many
f married
f metal
f missing
m more
m most
s new
f next
f nice
f noisy
s old
f open
f other
s our
f paper
f plastic
f poor
m quick
m quiet
f ready
f rich
s right (correct)
f right (direction)
m round
s sad
f same
s short
f silver
f single
m slow
s small
f soft
s sorry
m square
m straight
f strange
m strong
f sure
m tall
m thin
m thirsty
f tidy
m tired
s ugly
f unfriendly
f unhappy
f untidy
f warm
m weak

m well
m wet
m windy
m worse
m worst
m wrong
s young
s your

DETERMINERS

s a/an
m a lot of
m all
m another
m any
m every
f much
s my
s no
s some
s that
s the
s their
s these
s this
s those

ADVERBS

m a lot
s again
f ago
m all right
f already
f also
m always
f anywhere
f away
m badly
m before
m carefully
m down
m downstairs
f early
f ever
f everywhere
f far
f fast
f hard
s here
m how much
m how often
m inside
f just
m last
f late

f later
m loudly
m more
m most
f much
f near
f never
s not
s now
f nowhere
f of course (not)
m off
m often
m on
f once
m only
m out
m outside
f over
f perhaps
m quickly
m quietly
m slowly
f so
m sometimes
f somewhere
f soon
f still
f straight on
f suddenly
m then
s there
s today
f together
f tomorrow
f tonight
f too
f twice
m up
m upstairs
f usually
s very
m well
m when
f yet

PREPOSITIONS

m about
m above
f across
m after
s at
m before
s behind
m below

s between
m by
m down
f during
f far
f for
f from
s in
m in (time)
s in front of
m inside
f into
s like
f near
s next to
s of
m off
s on
m on (time)
m opposite
m outside
f over
f past
f since
f through
s to
s under
f until
s with
f without

PRONOUNS

m all
f anyone
f anything
† each
f else
f enough
f everyone
f everything
s he
s her
s hers
s him
s his
s I
s it
s its
s me
m mine
m more
m most
f no-one
m nothing
m ours

s she
f someone
m something
s that
m theirs
s them
s these
s they
s this
s those
s us
s we
m which
s you
s your
m yours

CONJUNCTIONS

s and
m because
m but
f if
s or
f so
m than
m then
m when

VERBS

Irregular:
s be
f begin
f break
f bring
f burn
m buy
s can/cannot/can't
s catch
m catch (a bus)
m choose
m come
f cut
s do/don't
s draw
s drink
s eat
f end
f fall
f fall over
f feel (like)
s find
s fly
f forget
f get
f get (off/on/to)

m get (un)dressed
m get up
s give
s go
f go out
f going to
s have (got)
m have (got) to
s have a bath
s have a drink/food
m have a party
m have a shower
m have a wash
f hear
s hit
m hurt
s know
s learn
f leave
f let
f lie down
f lose
f make
f may
m mean
f meet
f might
m must
s put
m put on
s read
s ride
s run
s say
s see
f sell
† send
f should
s sing
s sit (down)
s sleep
f smell (like) tr + intr
f speak
s spell
s stand (up)
f steal
s swim
f swing
m take
m take a bus
m take off
m take pictures
f take time
f teach
s tell
m think

31

s throw
s understand
m wake up
s wear
f will
f win
f won't
s write

Regular:

s add
f agree
s answer
f arrive
s ask
f ask for
f believe
s bounce
f brush
f burn
f call (what's x called?)
f camp
m carry
s clean
m climb
s close
s colour
f comb
m cook
s cross
m cry
m dance
f decide
f end
s enjoy
f explain
f fetch
f finish
m fish
f follow
f glue

f guess
f happen
f hate
m help
m hop
s jump
s kick
m laugh
s learn
s like
s listen (to)
s live
s look
s look (at)
f look (for)
f look (like)
s love
f mind
f mix
m move
m need
s open
s paint
s phone
s pick up
s play (with)
s point
s point to
f post
f prefer
f pull
f push
f race
m rain
f remember
m sail
f score
m shop
m shout
s show

m skate
f ski
m skip
f sledge
m snow
f sound (like)
s start
f stay
s stop
f study
s talk
f taste (like)
s test
f thank
s tick
f tidy
s try
f turn
f turn (off/on)
f use
f visit
m wait
s walk
s want
m wash
s watch
f whisper
f whistle
f wish
m work

INTERROGATIVE

m What's the matter?
m Why?
m When?
s Which? (Which is Ann?)
f Which? (Which snowman has Harry made?)